WITHDRAWN

D0239633

Lifelines 17

NEWMAN COLLEGE
BARTLEY GREEN
BIRMINGHAM, 32.

CLASS 720·9420314

ACCESSION 50200

AUTHOR Pug

Pugin

*An illustrated life of
Augustus Welby Northmore Pugin*

1812–1852

John Glen Harries

Shire Publications Ltd.

Contents

ACKNOWLEDGEMENTS

The author and publishers wish to thank the following for providing the photographs on the pages indicated: A. E. Bristow 2 and 7; Radio Times Hulton Picture Library 14, 27 (upper and lower) and 30; Royal Institute of British Architects 4. The illustrations by Pugin appearing on pages 11, 18, 21, 24, 41 and 45 were selected from books in the possession of B. Weinreb Architectural Books Ltd.; that on page 38 was provided by the Victoria and Albert Museum. The cover design is by Michael Hadley.

Copyright © 1973 by John Glen Harries. First published November 1973. ISBN 0 85263 204 5. All rights reserved. No part of this publication may be reproduced or transmitted in any form or by any means, electronic or mechanical, including photocopy, recording or any information storage and retrieval system, without permission in writing from the publishers, Shire Publications Ltd., 12B Temple Square, Aylesbury, Bucks., U.K.

Printed by Maund and Irvine Ltd., Tring, Herts.

Opposite: Augustus Welby Northmore Pugin (1812—1852). This memorial statue is one of some 170 figures depicting men famous in the arts and sciences that can be seen round the base of the Albert Memorial in Kensington.

The formative years

Pugin's life was short, lasting only forty years, and yet it contains within it elements of pain and tragedy, of comedy, of high spirits, of warmth and greatness, and of indomitable will. We see these elements unfold, even explode, with unusual rapidity and force. Pugin said when he was near death that he had performed the work of one hundred years in forty, and that it had worn him out; indeed, in his private life he seems to have led three lives in the space of one. The source of this consuming activity was present in his childhood, but though we may now realise this, and though others may have had some inkling of it at the time, we are driven to reflect how gently a torrent may begin, and how uncertain is its passage.

FAMILY BACKGROUND AND EARLY WORK

Augustus Welby Northmore Pugin came of an old and aristocratic family, though there is doubt as to whether its origins were in Switzerland, France, or even England, and its aristocracy was not given official recognition. But this background shaped Pugin's temperament, and enabled him to deal on equal terms with his clients.

His father, Auguste-Charles, Comte de Pugin, came to England in the time of Louis XVI, almost unable to speak English, and had to start from scratch. He worked in John Nash's studio, and having ability as a water-colourist, was quickly promoted. He helped Nash with his work in Gothic, an idiom strange to Nash, but natural to Auguste Pugin, and through publishing his own drawings, which were thorough and workmanlike, he achieved some fame which enabled him to collaborate, often in an unacknowledged way, with leading architects who needed assistance in the new style. Though he

Opposite: Augustus Welby Pugin painted by L. R. Herbert.

5

never set up his own architectural practice, Pugin's father was influential in establishing Gothic as more than a pasteboard approximation, and eventually in forming his son's tastes and abilities.

In 1802, this 'amiable and able' man married Catherine Welby, the daughter of a Temple barrister, and member of an 'old and distinguished' Lincolnshire family. She was attractive, literary, quick-witted and intense. Augustus Welby Pugin was their only child, born on 1st March 1812 at their house in Store Street, near Bedford Square, London.

He was delicate as a child, and was not sent to boarding-school but to Christ's Hospital, the Bluecoat School, as a day-boy. He was quick to learn, precocious, and by turns reserved and pugnacious, though the general impression was of a 'gentle and refined' character. He had, however, a high-spirited sense of humour, which emerged in the caricatures with which he entertained the pupils his father took. This sense of humour was a godsend. Pugin's mother was a complicated woman. She was kind and protective towards her son, and encouraged him in his creative activities, and she was devoted to her sister. But she was also a tough woman, being scornful of Pugin's inability to dress himself as a boy, and she inflicted a Spartan regime on the household, insisting on punctuality, early rising, silence at meal times and incessant industry. As time went on this became more oppressive. She followed the promptings of a religious zeal, and in her own self-denial appeared willing to sacrifice others to the same cause. Thus kindness was mixed with strong calls to duty, and resignation with a permanent agitation. The fact is that she suffered from ill health, and as well as being a force within her family, she was also rather puzzling to it.

Pugin, however, often used to say 'how happy I am! Nobody can be happier than I' — we can draw our own conclusions from this. Being inventive, he was allowed by his father to make architectural drawings and sketches rather than measured plans and was not subject to the drudgery inflicted upon his father's pupils. This was relieved by architectural tours, which extended to the continent as Auguste Pugin became more prosperous. His wife and son sometimes joined him — they did on a tour made to Paris in 1824. By this stage Pugin was able to help his father with books such as *Paris and its Environs* (published 1828–31), for which the son did 'more than three parts' of the

6

Store Street, near Bedford Square, London, where Pugin was born on 1st March 1812. His father worked as a water-colourist for John Nash and was influential in establishing Gothic.

work. He was also, although only just twelve, developing an obsessive interest in churches: 'When he heard that you left Beverley without seeing the churches, he declared, had he been with you, you would have found him the most restive animal you ever posted with; nor whip, nor spurs, nor anything else would have got him on before seeing those churches.' This interest, born of his father's dedication to Gothic, nurtured in his own drawings of Westminster Abbey and set glowing into life by the legends of the middle ages, existed as a kind of prelude to adolescence – but in this case survived it.

Pugin was not just a dreamer. When he was fourteen he undertook a formidable task with the permission of the fifth Earl of Jersey – a survey of Rochester Castle involving much measurement, drawing of imagined reconstruction, excavation, treasure-hunting and risk. Energy and romance were given full rein, and yet were combined with attention to detail: three of the abiding characteristics of Pugin's mind and architecture. Pugin was helped by one of his father's pupils, Benjamin Ferrey, who later wrote a biography of both father and son. Pugin had already studied the Tower of London and his idea was to emulate his father, and produce a book illustrating castles.

When he was fifteen Pugin was in the Print Room of the British Museum when a member of the firm of Rundell and Bridge (goldsmiths) saw a copy he was making of one of Dürer's works, and offered him his first job – designing plate. Pugin accepted, and did the job very well. He was also entrusted by his father with the task of designing Gothic furniture for George IV at Windsor Castle, and he performed the work with enthusiasm. While at Windsor he met George Dayes, who worked as a scene-shifter at Covent Garden Theatre, and he took Pugin along with him one night.

Here, in the scenery of the theatre, was a world of illusion, composed apparently of historical and architectural accuracy. And yet it was not yet historically accurate, and this jarred on Pugin's sense. He studied the craft of scenery production with Grieve's the scene-painters, making both suggestions and improvements, and installed a model theatre in the top floor of his parents' house in Great Russell Street; he was soon taken on at Covent Garden as a designer. When he was nineteen he produced spectacular and authentic sets for *Kenilworth*. Once again, Pugin had shown his knack of being in the right place at the right time, and his talent had now launched him on a promising career.

WORKS AND WOES

By the time Pugin was twenty, however, he was beset by difficulties – so much so that in 1832 his mother wrote: 'alas, alas! Look over the six years which have passed since that period (when he carried out the survey of Rochester Castle), and we find a whole life of woe, such as is rarely experienced by the generality of men, huddled into it. From his works and his woes he has already experienced a long life, and when he dies he will not die without some dignity, and have his name perpetuated.'

There had been a brief and ill-documented period in 1830 when he is supposed to have bought a boat, sailed to the continent on sketching and collecting trips, and eventually been shipwrecked near Leith in Scotland. If this was so, it must have represented a life of adventure and release from the confining, aesthetic world of home.

But then two events had happened to darken the scene. He set up a business in Hart Street, Covent Garden, to provide carved Gothic detail to order, and to train masons in the art of medieval stone-carving. After an initial success, this venture had failed, and he was unable to afford to rent the workshops. Carving of the type he specialised in was in demand, because the Gothic Revival was gathering momentum, but Pugin had no head for business. He was thrown in the sponging-house, though he was rescued from it by his aunt, Miss Selina Welby, was later able to pay off all his debts, and was cured of business ventures of this sort. This had been a worrying predicament, but not, like the second event, an overwhelming one.

This was the death of Pugin's first wife. While he was still in business he had met Anne Garnet, a relative of Edward Dayes. After a brief engagement they had married in 1831 – a mere folly in the eyes of his parents, with whom they went to live. But Anne Pugin 'showed a most affectionate regard, and exercised a beneficial influence over' Pugin and helped to see him through the business crisis. She died when she was eighteen after giving birth to her only child in May 1832, and is buried at Christchurch in Hampshire.

To us she is a rather shadowy figure. There is an air both of pathos and of slight theatricality in the two epitaphs to her. One is on her grave, where she is called 'the beloved wife of Augustus Welby Northmore de Pugin'; the other is on Pugin's watch, and reads: '*This day, May 27th, 1832, my dearest Anne died unto this world, but lived unto God*'. But Pugin's theatricality only ever emphasised the truth. Anne's death was 'a fearful blow to his sensitive mind' and throughout his life Pugin kept a death-mask of Anne, a cast of one of her hands, and an unfinished piece of needlework intended for her child. These things were only discovered at Pugin's own death.

Again the events of Pugin's life followed in rapid succession. In the same year his father died, and four months afterwards, his mother. On the strength of his inheritance, and of the continuing sales of his father's books, Pugin went to live in Salisbury. There he married his second wife, Louisa, and not long after that he moved with his daughter Anne and his new wife to Ramsgate, where his aunt Selina Welby lived. Pugin was now reasonably well off, and free to travel – though with the object of working and studying, as well as enjoying himself.

REACTION

Pugin did work incessantly, partly to forget his troubles, partly through sheer temperament, and partly through fascination with Gothic. He now considered himself among the 'real Gothic men' and even hoped for 'a little Gothic boy or girl' from his wife, with which he was duly presented in 1834 – Edward Welby Pugin.

In the records of his work and observations at this time there is an extreme excitement, caused by the beauty of the buildings he saw and by their mistreatment at the hands of the Puritans, the clergy and 'restorers', especially James Wyatt (1746–1813): 'Maddened by the sight I rushed to the cathedral (of Hereford); but horror! dismay! the villain Wyatt had been there, the west front was his. Need I say more?' 'Yes, this monster of architectural depravity – this pest of cathedral architecture – had been here: need I say more?' He did say more about the patrons of restoration: 'A few years ago a meeting of the fashionables of Malvern was called to subscribe towards the repairs of the delapidated building (of Malvern Abbey), and by the help of raffles, &c., a few pounds were collected. Two hodfulls of mortar were got to repair the church, and the remainder of the money expended in putting in a window of the aisle the arms of the subscribers in stained glass, with their names in full, a monument of folly and arrogance . . . The church itself is in dreadful repair; fall it must, and all that is to be hoped is, that in its fall it may annihilate those whose duty it was to have restored it . . . '

He attacks too, though in a light-hearted manner, the memorial tablets with which churches were embellished by his friend Osmond, who received all this correspondence. Inviting him to look at Wells Cathedral with him, Pugin writes: ' . . . without you make a pilgrimage to this shrine you will never obtain absolution for the number of *blisters* you have been the instrument of fixing and polluting against ancient arts'. Urging Osmond to join him on 'a nine month's journey in Normandy and the Low Countries', he says 'Leave your *blisters*, leave your Doric porticoes, leave all and follow me'.

Pugin's writing is vivid and emphatic, as in his description of Birmingham as 'that most detestable of all detestable places . . . where Greek buildings and smoking chimneys, Radicals and Dissenters are blended together.' His reactions are always strong and interesting, and in some cases he found them almost distracting: 'If you want to be delighted, if you want to be astonished, if you want to be half mad, as I at present am, for God's sake come over to Wells . . . Gothic for ever!' 'I have been at the Cathedral (of Ely) all the morning. How I am delighted! how I am pained!' Everything is superlative: 'splendid specimens of sculpture'; 'the finest tower of the kind in England' (Taunton); 'one of the most perfect castles I have ever seen' (Chepstow); 'the stained glass (at Lichfield Cathedral) . . . is without exception the most beautiful I have ever seen' – and so on. If ever a man was possessed by a ruling passion it was Pugin – though he also had an independent mind: while giving Tintern Abbey full credit for its good points, he goes against popular opinion by saying that 'as a building, it is anything but admirable'.

Out of Pugin's visits to British cathedrals, which he called his 'travels in search of the beautiful', emerged not only a stream of letters, some of them finely illustrated, but also 'several new books' – including the four parts of *Ornaments of the XVth and XVIth Centuries*. As he himself remarked, he worked 'without ceasing'.

Three tankards by Pugin which appear in his book 'Gothic Ornaments of the 15th and 16th Centuries'.

CONVERSION

While making these journeys, Pugin was gradually becoming convinced that Roman Catholicism was the true religion. The process by which he was led to this conviction has aroused some doubt, but it seems perfectly clear, if rather devious. From associating Catholicism with 'racks, faggots, and fires, idolatry, sin-purchase, &c.' Pugin came to see it as the creator of the architectural beauty he so ardently admired. But although he admired it, the spirit of this medieval work was 'unintelligible' to him at that time and it was not until he delved into the rites and doctrines of Catholicism that all became apparent, and the Roman Catholic Church emerged in his mind as the great and constant civilising force of England. By now the matter had ceased to be one of aesthetics, or of study, and had become one of emotion – though all three were blended in a unity presumably beyond the comprehension of his detractors. The architectural, historic, liturgical and spiritual aspects of Roman Catholicism answered perfectly to Pugin's own needs, and to his gifts.

All Pugin's statements about his conversion are to be seen against this background, and the exercise dispels any idea of shallowness or insincerity on his part. Thus he says: 'I learned the truths of the Catholic religion in the crypts of the old cathedrals of Europe. I sought for these truths in the modern church of England, and found that since her separation from the centre of Catholic unity she had little truth, and no life; so without being acquainted with a single Priest, through God's mercy, I resolved to enter His Church'; and again: 'I feel perfectly convinced the Roman Catholic Church is the only true one, and the only one in which the grand and sublime style of church architecture can ever be restored'.

Pugin was never afraid of the sublime, in art or in religion, but in spite of this he speaks of the 'simple truth' of Catholicism and counted himself 'an humble, but I trust faithful member' of its Church. The last word on the subject should be left to him: 'I therefore hope that in Christian charity my conversion will not any longer be attributed solely to my admiration of architectural excellence: for although I have freely acknowledged that my attention was first directed through it to the subject, yet I must distinctly state, that so important a change was not effected in me, but by the most

This engraving from Ferrey's biography of Pugin is possibly an early sketch for Pugin's Salisbury home, St Marie's Grange, 'compleat in every part in the antient style'.

powerful reasons, and that after long and earnest examination.' Roman Catholicism was unpopular in many quarters, and it was still a rather obscure religion. It had not yet been brought to prominence by the Oxford Movement, and by Newman's *Tracts for the Times.* In adopting it, Pugin renounced the chance of restoring the Anglican churches he admired – but he gained a driving force that informed both his work and his life.

Pugin now decided to settle in Salisbury. In 1834 he had helped to restore a medieval guildhall there, the Hall of John Halle, and 'in all his travels' Pugin 'had never seen a pleasanter city'. In 1835 he bought two acres of land near the river Avon, and set about building a house which he called St Marie's Grange. He gave it a chapel, a cross and a belfry, and a plaque saying in Gothic script: *Hanc Domum cum capella edificavit Augustus de Pugin† sub invoc(atione) beatae Mariae† anno christ(i) 1835† laus deo†.* Pugin said that the house would be 'the only modern building that is compleat in every part in the antient style', and it does recall the fortified manors of the

13

King Edward VI School, Birmingham. Pugin gave Charles Barry much assistance in the plans for this building, submitting many drawings for Gothic detail and designing the furniture for the interior.

fifteenth century. It also shows some continental influence with its pointed roofs, turrets and bell-cote, and its dark, mullioned windows. Pugin demanded 'enormously thick walls and deep splays to the windows, strong oak bars for fastenings, and not a scrap of plaster or battening where such materials were usually put.' It had three other unusual features: it had only a winding turret stair; it was cellular in construction (there was no hallway or passage); and it had a moat and drawbridge because Pugin was afraid of fire. It was a snug, romantic, beautifully made and rather eccentric house, though perhaps a little close and sombre.

Patrons and friends

THE HOUSES OF PARLIAMENT

At St Marie's Grange Pugin settled down to hard and solitary work; to architectural study, to augmenting his collection of books, antiquities and pictures, and to completing the plates of his *Ornaments of the XVth and XVIth Centuries*, for publication by the London firm of Ackermann and Co. At the same time, 1835, he designed a church for James Gillespie Graham. He did some work for Charles Barry, contributing Gothic detail to Barry's designs for the King Edward VI Grammar School in Birmingham – and this began a great architectural collaboration. In October 1834 the old Houses of Parliament had been burnt down and a competition was opened for the design of a replacement. Pugin helped Barry with his entry, again by taking almost sole charge of the detail, and in February 1836 it was announced that Barry had won the competition.

It was a condition of the competition that the style of the new building should be either Gothic or Elizabethan and it was the first major secular and public building to be cast in this revived style. The competition elicited more than one thousand drawings, among them being an entry by James Gillespie Graham which Pugin had helped with. Pugin wrote: 'Is not this a regular joke? Here are these two rivals competing for one prize, and I am making the designs for both.' For some months, Pugin spent much of his time on Barry's plans, and Barry himself became ill through overwork and lack of sleep. Barry, however, received £8,500 as a premium, before his architectural fees were paid, and of this Pugin got only £400. This was an unjust distribution, but Pugin was pressed for money to settle the debts he had contracted in his carving business, and he was certain of getting this. He was paid, too, for his later contributions. Had he wanted more money, Pugin could have entered the competition himself, but he felt that as a Catholic

15

he would stand no chance of winning, and also that the requirements of the commission were beyond him. He fully acknowledged the grasp of broad planning that enabled Barry to accomplish this enormous task: 'Besides, I could not have made that plan; it was Barry's own; he was good at such work – excellent; but the various requirements conveyed by the plan, which were not of art, and above all the Fine Art Commissioners, would have been too much for me.'

The part played in the design of the Houses of Parliament was a matter of expediency, but it also represented a happy adjustment between the major architectural virtues of each man: between Barry's Classical command of grand and simple volume, and Pugin's brilliance as a designer of Gothic detail. Pugin realised the nature of this contrast, but did not like it, and later dismissed the building as 'All Grecian, Sir; Tudor details on a classic body.' Pugin did not like, either, the fact that he, a relatively unknown architect, was being used by Barry, an established one, and yet given no credit for it. Barry was very sympathetic, with his entreaties that Pugin should not let his health suffer 'from excess of application', and with his 'best wishes for Mrs Pugin's early recovery' from one of her recurring bouts of illness. He was quick to praise Pugin's ability and expressed astonishment at his *'50-horse power of creation.'* But still, Pugin's part in the project was almost concealed, and while for a time he connived at this, partly out of the sheer interest of the work, it gradually began to irritate him. Add to this that Barry gave work on Pugin's designs to a man trained by Pugin, rather than to Pugin himself; that Pugin probably implied that his own architectural sense was superior to Barry's; and that Pugin's contribution seemed to be complete, and you have the makings of a split that was desired on both sides. It came in 1837, and lasted for seven years.

On top of all this, Pugin had to contend with domestic and health worries, having often been ill in the past, generally in some way connected with overwork. When he was fifteen, for example, he had collapsed while visiting Notre Dame in Paris. Now, in the middle of the competition work, he suffered a temporary attack of blindness. His wife, too, was in bad health. This, and the fact that in 1836 she had another baby, contributed towards their leaving St Marie's Grange in 1837, barely two years after it had been built. Pugin decided to put it

16

on the market in 1840, but because it was unusual, it was hard to sell.

Before this, and in spite of his original declaration of humility, Pugin had become a champion of the Catholic faith. He 'officiated as an acolyte', and engaged in 'the thick of Catholic controversy', especially with A. W. Hakewill, who had the temerity to compare the great London Gothic buildings to 'noxious weeds', and Classic architecture to a flower. Not only this, but in 1836 Pugin produced the book called *Contrasts*. Because of its individuality and its aggressively Catholic stance, Pugin was forced to publish it himself and lost a lot of money in the process – but it made his name.

'CONTRASTS'

Contrasts was subtitled 'a parallel between the noble edifices of the fourteenth and fifteenth centuries and similar buildings of the present day; shewing the present decay of taste: Accompanied by appropriate Text.' This makes its subject plain enough. In the first edition the 'present decay' was imputed almost solely to Protestantism – a fact which was satirised in a *Song on Pugin's Contrasts* 'By Mr McCann, an Irishman':

> OH! have you seen the work just out
>   By Pugin, the great builder?
> 'Architect'ral Contrasts' he's made out
>   Poor Protestants to bewilder.
> The Catholic Church, she never knew –
>   Till Mr Pugin taught her,
> That orthodoxy had to do
>   At all with bricks and mortar.
>
> But now it's clear to one and all,
>   Since he's published his lecture,
> No church is Catholic at all
>   Without Gothic architecture.
> In fact, he quite turns up his nose
>   At any style that's racent,
> The Gracian, too, he plainly shows
>   Is wicked and ondacent.

A second edition of *Contrasts*, revised and expanded to over double the length of the first, was published five years later in

NEW CHVRCH
OPEN COMPETITION

TO YOVTHFVL VNEMPLOYED AND ASPIRING ARCHITECTS

FOR THE BEST DESIGN
FIVE POVNDS
THE 4 NEXT BEST
IN PROPORTION

A CHVRCH TO CONTAIN 8000 SIT-TINGS
GOTHIC or ELISABETHAN
ESTIMATE MVST NOT EXCEED £1500. AND STYLE PLAIN

EACH CANDIDATE
MVST SEND
4 ELEVATIONS 3 SECTIONS
PLANS AND 3 PERSPECTIVE
VIEWS

ELEGANT TERMINATIONS CHEAP
DESIGNING TAVGHT IN 6 LESSONS
GOTHIC SEVERE GREEK
AND THE
MIXED STYLES
ON WEDNESDAY AND FRIDAY EVENINGS
FROM 6 to 8 OCLOCK

GOTHIC CHIMNEYS FROM 10 TO 30 S

READY MADE BALVSTRADES all SIZES

TEMPLE OF TASTE, AND ARCHITECTVRAL REPOSITORY

COMPO FRONTS FORWARDED TO ALL PARTS of the KINGDOM
BY STEAM CONVEYANCE ON THE SHORTEST NOTICE

DESIGNS WANTED

A MOORISH FISH MARKET WITH A LITERARY ROOM OVER

AN EGYPTIAN MARINE VILLA

A CASTELATED TVRNPIKE GATE

A GIN TEMPLE IN THE BARONIAL STYLE

A DISSENTING CHAPEL IN A PLAIN STYLE TO SERVE OCCASIONALY FOR A LECTURE OR READING ROOM

A MONVMENT TO BE PLACED IN WESTMINSTER ABBEY A COLOSSAL FIGVRE IN WHILNDOO STYLE WOVLD BE PREFERRED AND NO REGARD NEED BE PAID TO LOCALITY

A SAXON CIGAR DIVAN

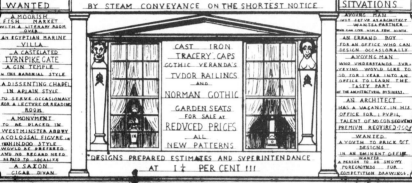

CAST IRON TRACERY CAPS
GOTHIC VERANDA'S
TVDOR RAILINGS
AND
NORMAN GOTHIC
GARDEN SEATS
FOR SALE AT
REDVCED PRICES
ALL
NEW PATTERNS

"DESIGNS PREPARED ESTIMATES AND SVPERINTENDANCE
AT 1¼ PER CENT !!!

PLACES and SITVATIONS

A YOVNG MAN MVST SETVP AS A ARCHITECT WHO CAN GIVE HIM A FEW HINTS

AN ERRAND BOY FOR AN OFFICE WHO CAN DESIGN OCCASIONALLY

A YOVNG MAN WHO VNDERSTANDS SVRVEYING WOVLD LIKE TO GO FOR 1 YEAR INTO AN OFFICE TO LEARN THE TASTY PART OF THE ARCHITECTVRAL BVSINESS

AN ARCHITECT HAS A VACANCY IN HIS OFFICE FOR 1 PVPIL TALENT OF NO CONSEQVENT PREMIVM REQVIRED 700l

WANTED A YOVTH TO PRICK OFF DESIGNS IN AN EMINENT OFFICE

WANTED A PERSON TO DO SHOWY FOREGROVNDS FOR COMPETITION DRAWINGS

MECHANICKS INSTITVTE
A LECTVRE ON ANTIDELVVIAN BABYLONIAN CREEK ROMAN AND GOTHIC ARCHITECTVRE BY Mr WASH PLASTERER who goes out 3 day work on moderate terms

ARCHITECTVRAL OFFICE

ATTENDANCE FROM 10 till 4 EVERY DAY AND ON SVNDAYS AFTER CHVRCH

A LARGE QVANTITY OF GOTHIC CORNICES
JVST PRESSED OVT FROM 6^d PER YARD

BVILDINGS OF EVERY DESCRIPTION ALTERED INTO
GOTHIC or GRECIAN
ON MODERATE TERMS
TERRACE FRONTS DESIGNED

DESIGNS DONE IN THIS STYLE

A TRIVMPHAL ARCH

SHORTLY WILL BE PVBLISHED
ARCHITECTVRE MADE EASY
OR EVERY MAN HIS OWN ARCHITECT
BY WHICH
GENTLEMEN AMATEVRS MAY EASILY ACQVIRE EVERY INFORMATION RESPECTING
DESIGN AND PRACTICE

JVST PVBLISHED
THE DESIGNERS RECKONER
BY WHICH
THE ORNAMENTS AND STYLE OF CHVRCHES
MAY BE REGVLATED FROM 2 POVNDS PER SITTING

MECHANICKS INSTITVTE
A LECTVRE ON A NEW DESIGNING MACHINE CAPABLE OF MAKING 1000 CHANGES WITH THE SAME SET OF ORNAMENTS BY A COMPOSITION MAKER

HOVSE OF CALL FOR STVDENTS

2^d HAND DESIGNS BOVGHT AND BEST PRICE ALLOWED FOR WASTE PAPER

A LARGE ASSORTMENT OF REJECTED DESIGNS
SELLING CONSIDERABLY VNDER PRIME COST

THIS ILLVSTRATION
OF THE PRACTISE OF ARCHITECTVRE IN THE 19 CENTVRY ON NEW IMPROVED AND CHEAP PRINCIPLE
IS DEDICATED WITHOVT PERMISSION TO
THE TRADE

1841 by Charles Dolman of London. In this, Pugin with rather more perception shifted the blame to 'the decayed state of faith throughout Europe in the fifteenth century'.

Whichever the edition, *Contrasts* is a striking book. We may not agree with all the contrasts: Nash's All Souls, Langham Place, London, seems to us a compact and elegant building, even if it is not as majestic as the church of St Mary Redcliffe, Bristol. The house that Sir John Soane designed for himself now seems an original and distinguished one, as impressive in its way as the house in the Rue de l'horloge, Rouen. Pugin also idealises some aspects of medieval life, such as the 'antient poor house', though the nineteenth-century version is bleak and brutal enough.

But if Pugin's judgement sometimes fails him in considering contemporary work, he was solidly right about Gothic buildings – and he was probably always right in the matter of religious feeling. So there is much truth in the contrasts, and besides that, a great deal of wit and entertaining detail. His satires on 'The New Square Style' he connected with Soane and Sir Robert Smirke, and on Classical and Gothic Revival monuments, are worthy of *Punch*, which incidentally satirised him in due course. But best of all is the plate dedicated to 'The Trade'. Whatever the rights and wrongs of Pugin's case, *Contrasts* is, in execution, in its light and shade, and in its vigour, a work of true originality. As well as bringing Pugin notoriety, it gave impetus to the Gothic Revival and helped to arouse concern over the deterioration and destruction of old buildings.

SCARISBRICK

In 1837 Pugin undertook his first major independent architectural commission, the refurbishing and extension of the sixteenth-century family home of the Scarisbricks. Charles Scarisbrick was a Catholic and a bachelor, at that time 36 years old, and as Nathaniel Hawthorne remarked, 'a very eccentric man' who spent 'all his time at the secluded hall, which stands in the midst of mosses and marshes' in Lancashire. He was also an

---

Opposite: from 'Contrasts' comes this 'illustration of the practise of architecture in the 19th century on new improved and cheap principles'. 'Contrasts' was written to outline the decay of architectural taste and is directed against Protestantism.

immensely wealthy owner of property, and shared Pugin's architectural tastes.

The opportunity provided by Scarisbrick's commission was a splendid one for an architect twenty-five years old, and Pugin took full advantage of it. He converted the crumbling house into a Gothic Revival mansion, complete with great hall and clock tower. The exterior is harmonious. It is enriched by bay windows and oriels, but remains simple and dignified in its massing. Into the interior Pugin let abundant light and with the help of such men as John Hardman (Junior) of Birmingham and J. G. Crace he filled the rooms with decoration of the highest quality. There was a chance in the carved and moulded work of fireplaces and doors, for example, to use his knowledge of the more elaborate forms of medieval and continental design, and to indulge in great extravagance. He enjoyed it, and Charles Scarisbrick demanded it as a fitting expression of his family's worth.

Scarisbrick was mindful of the seriousness of his responsibility, and placed about the house are various texts: 'Ye will show kindness to my Father's house'; 'I have raised up the ruins, and I have builded it as in the days of old'; 'Every house is builded by some man, but He that builded all is God'; 'It is vain for you to rise up early, to sit up late, to eat the bread of sorrows, for so He giveth His beloved sleep'; and 'For He that is mighty hath done great things for me and holy is His name. Alleluia.'

Although Pugin worked on the building until 1845, he did not live to see its completion. Neither did Charles Scarisbrick: he died in 1860, seated alone before a fire in the dining-room of the vast and cold house he had created through his own determination and the ability of a great architect. When the building was completed, it was not in the way that Pugin had intended. The work was eventually taken in hand by Scarisbrick's widowed sister, Ann, who inherited the house when she was seventy-two, and she gave the job to Pugin's son, Edward Welby. He was allowed to do as he liked and he let his decorative fancy run riot, so that there is a marked contrast between the eastern portion, which he designed, and his father's

---

Opposite: an ink drawing (c. 1837) by Pugin for the fireplace in the south room, old wing, Scarisbrick Hall. Pugin transformed this house into a Gothic Revival mansion.

work. The initials of Ann Scarisbrick and, by courtesy, of Pugin himself also run riot throughout the building, and complete this strange house built by strange people.

LORD SHREWSBURY

Pugin now decided to concentrate on church architecture. In 1836 he had received a letter from Doctor Daniel Rock which praised him highly for his *Ornaments of the XVth and XVIth Centuries*. This was a fortunate occurrence, for not only was Dr Rock one of the most learned scholars of the day, he was also chaplain at Alton Towers, near Cheadle in Staffordshire, to the Earl of Shrewsbury. Pugin sent a copy of *Contrasts* to Alton Towers, the three men met and got on well, and Pugin found a new world of possibilities open to him – such was the power of wealth and of influence in Catholic circles, and Lord Shrewsbury possessed both, giving immense sums for the provision of churches and various charities. By nature he was calm and diligent, though capable of decisive action when necessary, and he lived a relatively simple life amid 'the princely towers and enchanted gardens of Alton'.

Much of the architectural work at Alton had been done by local architects, but from now until his death in 1852 Pugin added several distinguished features, including decorations to the chapel, the 'Pugin staircase' and lastly, in the late 1840s, the dining-hall. There was some dispute over this, as Lord Shrewsbury was contemplating a design which, Pugin wrote, was 'fit only for a hotel'. He continued: 'I never proposed anything for *mere effect*. I know my design was quite right . . . as regards the hall, I have nailed my colours to the mast – a bay window, high open roof, lantern, two good fire-places, a great sideboard, screen, minstrel-gallery – *all or none*. I will not sell myself to do a wretched thing. Lady Shrewsbury told me, when I was last at Alton, that she would rather see the present room left, unless the new one was a truly fine work: and I am sure her ladyship is right.' Lady Shrewsbury's view of the matter prevailed, and the room was built as Pugin intended.

OSCOTT

Through Lord Shrewsbury and Dr Rock, in 1837 Pugin was appointed architect to St Mary's College, Oscott, near

22

Birmingham, thus ousting a Mr Potter of Lichfield from the post. Pugin worked at Oscott for two years, and stayed there from time to time at 9 St Bede's Passage. This was an important and satisfying period of his life, and he always looked back on it with pleasure. Pugin did a great deal of the decorative work at Oscott, and more particularly he extended and enriched the chapel begun by Mr Potter as 'a plain oblong building'. He added an apsidal sanctuary with a 'beautiful groined roof', and he added colour, in the altar, in the reredos with its Limoges enamels, in painted stone and wood, and in his own stained glass and heraldry — the first colour to appear in England, the *Oscotian* stated, 'after a century and a half of whitewash and false marbling'.

Pugin lived in a daze of activity and of intoxication at the coming, as he felt, of a new Catholic age. He did outside work, designing all kinds of church plate for John Hardman, who founded the Ecclesiastical Metal Works and who,

Pugin added several distinguished features to Alton Towers in Staffordshire and in addition to this work he made this contribution to the railways, Alton station.

In 'The True Principles of Pointed or Christian Architecture' Pugin mocks the builders of the 'Modern Castellated Mansion': '... drawbridges which will not draw up ... a bastion in which the butler cleans his plate: all is a mere mask'.

from 1838 onwards, was Pugin's partner in producing stained glass and metalwork. Within the College Pugin designed everything, from a lead cap for the bell-tower, a high wooden screen, and furniture (some of it for the museum he started) to iron ink-pots, various gowns and vestments 'made in London, by the costume makers of the Italian opera', and a great deal of church plate and devotional ornament: candlesticks – the paschal one, eleven feet high, and four brass ones which, together with a crucifix, he presented himself; a carved Madonna; a pax; and a pulpit. The list is endless, and is a measure of his affection for Oscott, as is the altar that he presented to the College in 1842.

This affection was certainly returned: Bishop Walsh paid tribute to his 'talents and zeal', to the 'solemnity' he had 'added to the religious ceremonies' and to his 'various other acts of kindness', while the students presented him with an address in appreciation of his efforts. As a result of this warm reception Pugin gained considerable confidence, and as early as 1837 he wrote: 'Could you but see me at Oscott you would hardly credit me to be the same individual that you remember *some years ago'.*

'TRUE PRINCIPLES'

Pugin was also Professor of Ecclesiastical Antiquities at Oscott, and in the middle of all this other activity he delivered a series of lectures which culminated, in 1841, in the publication of *The True Principles of Pointed or Christian Architecture.* This is Pugin's central statement of his architectural beliefs. Instead of being entirely systematic, it proceeds from conviction to conviction with passionate force. But it is a philosophical and mature work and the result of his own search for clarity and unity in architecture: 'In conclusion, Christian verity compels me to acknowledge that there are hardly any defects which I have pointed out ... which could not with propriety be illustrated by my own productions at some period of my professional career. Truth is only gradually developed in the mind, and is the result of long experience and deep investigation'. Earlier, speaking of current fashions in interior design, he writes: 'We find diminutive flying buttresses upon an arm chair; everything is crocketed with angular projections, innumerable mitres, sharp ornaments, and turreted extremities. A man who remains for any length of time in a modern Gothic room, and escapes without being wounded by some of its minutiæ, may consider himself extremely fortunate ... I have perpetrated many of these enormities in the furniture I designed some years ago for Windsor Castle. At that time I had not the least idea of the principles I am now explaining; all my knowledge of Pointed Architecture was confined to a tolerably good notion of details in the abstract; but these I employed with so little judgement or propriety, that, although the parts were correct and exceedingly well executed, collectively they appeared a complete burlesque of pointed design.'

Wit is used, but the intention of serious. It was 'to set forth and explain the true principles of Pointed or Christian Architecture, by the knowledge of which you may be enabled to test architectural excellence. The two great rules for design are these: 1st, that there should be no features about a building which are not necessary for convenience, construction, or propriety; 2nd, that all ornament should consist of enrichment of the essential construction of the building.' Pugin adds: 'In pure architecture the smallest detail should have a meaning or serve a purpose; and even the construction itself should vary with the material employed'; and 'the external and internal appearance of an edifice should be illustrative of, and in accordance with, the purpose for which it is destined.' These are the canons of craftsmanship, with which Pugin was involved long before it became a fashionable nineteenth-century cry with William Morris and others, and before it emerged in the twentieth century in ideas of functionalism and honesty. By going to the roots of tradition, and isolating principles applicable to nearly all architecture, Pugin was very much ahead of his time.

Pugin, however, did not think that these principles applied to all architecture, and his final extension of them was that they were enshrined in Catholic, pointed Gothic: 'Strange as it may appear at first sight, it is in pointed architecture alone that these great principles have been carried out.'

The principles gathered together in this way are used as a base from which to attack all forms of 'deception' or disguise in architecture and design, and all forms of redundancy in decoration. Thus modern abuses and ancient wrongs come within Pugin's scope. Fenders like castle battlements, tongs surmounted by saints, clocks like church towers, inkstands like staircase turrets, and light-shades like monumental crosses – as well as everything 'continually produced from those inexhaustible mines of bad taste, Birmingham and Sheffield' – are all attacked. But so is the roof of Henry VII's Chapel in Westminster Abbey, because the stone pendants are considered excessive.

Pugin's main onslaught was reserved for Classic, or 'Pagan', architecture which he saw as maladroit and dishonest. Shapes continued to be made in stone which had originally been devised for construction in wood, and, said Pugin, at St Paul's Cathedral 'one half of the edifice is built to conceal the other'. Pugin's attack is couched in an extremely lively and entertaining style, and reminds us of the high standard of nineteenth-century architectural writing. He is always outspoken: elsewhere he had said that in the stained glass designed by Sir Joshua Reynolds for New College, Oxford, the figures representing the Cardinal Virtues looked like 'third-rate actresses', and that two-thirds of the picture consisted of 'dirty brown clouds'. Pugin can be

The West window at New College, Oxford, by Sir Joshua Reynolds. Pugin complained that the figures looked like 'third-rate actresses'.

St Mary's College, Oscott, near Birmingham. Pugin worked here for two years, greatly enriching the chapel and designing everything within the college.

dogmatic and didactic but he is never simply negative in his approach. *True Principles* contains a strong positive element of praise and admiration for the things that did avoid 'modern paltry taste and paganism', and for the things that had always exemplified 'the Beautiful and the True'. Naïve as that last phrase may sound it goes with a view whose depth and sensitivity, as well as irony, place the book and Pugin himself beyond the charge often brought – of mere Gothic fanaticism.

MARCH-PHILLIPPS

In the same year as the connection with Oscott began, 1837, Pugin travelled extensively in France and the Low Countries, his wife and family moved to lodgings in Chelsea, and he made the acquaintance of a number of influential people. The most notable of these was Ambrose Lisle March-Phillipps. March-Phillipps, who later added 'de Lisle' to his surname, was the son of a Leicestershire squire, and was converted to Roman Catholicism when he was seventeen. He built the Leicestershire manor house of Grace Dieu for himself in 1833–34, and a prominent place was occupied by a chapel. This preserved the spirit and form of medieval worship: it had a rood screen, sumptuous vestments designed by Pugin, services were conducted in full, and the music was Gregorian chant. All this summed up what both March-Phillipps and Pugin longed for. The two became lifelong friends and later engaged in several joint endeavours, especially the foundation and building of the Cistercian monastery of Mount St Bernard in Leicestershire, and the advocacy of the old style in church vestments against great opposition – undertakings in which Lord Shrewsbury's money and influence were indispensible: so that the three formed a triumvirate of Catholic tradition. In 1838 and 1839 Pugin wrote with increasing vehemence in defence of Catholicism and against Protestantism.

Churches and cathedrals

DEVELOPING POWERS

|Pugin's architectural fortunes had changed now, and by 1838
he had received commissions for ten churches in England and
two in Ireland. |He worked very hard on these designs for the
next two years, so that in 1839 he could say 'I have now an
immense deal of business, and if I live on two or three years
shall have done something worth looking at'; and 'I have twice
as much as I can do, though I work early and late. Were I not
driven beyond my strength, you should not wait a moment'.
Pugin was overworking, often tired and ill, and had begun the
course that was to wear him out in thirteen years. But the
results were not, immediately, to his satisfaction.

|The first church to be opened, in August 1839, was St
Mary's, Uttoxeter, and Lord Shrewsbury attended the
ceremony. There followed St Augustine's, Solihull; Our Lady
and St Thomas of Canterbury, Dudley; St Anne's, Keighley; the
chapel of St Peter's College, Wexford; the parish church
attributed to Pugin at Bree, near Enniscorthy; St Marie's,
Southport; the church at Radford; and the first church designed
by Pugin, St James's, Reading – which was in uncharacteristic
Norman style. These were modest churches, aisleless, and with a
bell-cote rather than a tower. The one at Dudley, compact and
reasonably satisfying, cost £3,165 for example, and Pugin said
that Uttoxeter provided 'an instance that a Catholic church,
complete in every respect, may be erected for a very moderate
sum'. The stress in all these churches – and it was a stress about
which Pugin felt passionately – was first on the chancel and its
liturgical fittings, including an arched rood, then on the nave
and last on the exterior – with the result that the buildings
appear rather Spartan on the outside. The truth is that, in spite
of what he said about Uttoxeter, Pugin was not given enough
money to make these churches truly impressive and his plans
were often changed – two factors which, with a few exceptions,

The Cistercian monastery of Mount St Bernard, Leicestershire. This was one of several joint endeavours of Pugin and Ambrose Lisle March-Phillipps.

dogged him throughout his church-building career and caused him great distress. As they stand now, these churches have been changed almost out of recognition.

The first major church of Pugin's to be built was St Mary's, Derby, which was opened at the end of 1839. Again, money was limited and the site, as well as being north-south, was also narrow. But Pugin went all out for height and nobility and he achieved them, even though the graceful spire which would have made the church 200 feet tall was never built. The nave is lofty, the lines of the arcades and chancel arch continue in an unbroken sweep, and a splendid rood-arch and crucifix stand out against the shadow of the chancel, which is pierced with coloured lancets. The whole has an effect of great space and dignity. Contrary to Pugin's intentions, the stone has been painted, but even this cannot detract from the drama of the design.

Both the plate and fittings, made by John Hardman, and the vestments used at the opening were designed by Pugin. The vestments were in the authentic medieval style, and this led to the controversy already mentioned. Starting with the Right

Reverend John Briggs, Vicar Apostolic of Yorkshire, and taking in Bishop Baines on the way, a number of influential Catholics objected to the vestments because they departed from the pattern in use throughout the Roman Catholic Church, and a complaint was lodged with Propaganda accordingly. Propaganda's response was not unequivocal, but hints were dropped which Pugin took as a reproof. He was incensed, at the facts that his designs had been misrepresented to Rome as 'innovations', that the complainants were anonymous, and above all that they were in this small way working against attempts 'to restore religion to its antient dignity' instead of 'aiding the great work'. Awoken from his 'dreams of returning glory' Pugin was 'sick at heart'. He enlisted the help of March-Phillipps, who in turn appealed to Lord Shrewsbury. Propaganda took the matter no further, and after a period of disuse, the vestments were restored to use.

All this shows the developing conflict between two Catholic groups – the New Catholics, and the English Catholics supported by Pugin. The heat generated was not entirely over a few robes, therefore, but over different religious attitudes. Nevertheless, like many nineteenth-century religious controversies, the business reminds us that when men have no great matters to argue about they will argue about small ones.

Pugin's next major church was St Alban's, Macclesfield, which was designed at the end of 1838 and opened in 1841. The interior is imposing and dignified, though it does not give the same impression of soaring twilit space as St Mary's, Derby, in spite of the fact that the nave is eleven feet higher. This is because the church is also wider, the chancel arch lower relative to the arcades, and the arcades themselves broken by capitals. The result is an interior that seems more broadly based or down-to-earth, and more brightly-lit, though the chancel retains an air of richness and mystery. This is accentuated by a rood-screen, and a rood which appears to hover in the darkness scooped out by the chancel arch. This was the first rood-screen introduced by Pugin, and others followed at Dudley and Southport: Pugin indeed came to see rood-screens as an essential feature of interiors, separating the functions of chancel and nave, and thereby reinforcing the old splendours of religion – a view that was later to involve him once again in controversy. The exterior of the church is forthright, if a little

31

The frontispiece to 'An Apology for the Revival of Christian Architecture in England'. This was Pugin's last major book and in it he strives 'to place Christian architecture in its true position' while condemning the contemporary 'carnival of architecture' and all those who disparage Gothic.

ungainly. The tower is truncated, since it lacks the belfry-stage shown in the frontispiece to a book Pugin published in 1843, *An Apology for the Revival of Christian Architecture in England.*

At the same time as St Alban's was being built work was progressing on another church, St Wilfrid's at Hulme in Manchester. Enforced economy and a demand for size made this rather a barn of a building on the outside (it is of brick and was not given the tower shown in the frontispiece to the *Apology*) and the impression is carried on inside by the rafters, which are bare and open, though they make quite a delicate framework. But it is an honest and workmanlike building, and the resources have been handled in a coherent way so as to place the emphasis on the chancel. In contrast to Pugin's usual arrangement, this glows with light in the midst of a darkened church.

ACHIEVEMENT

1839 saw the start of some of Pugin's largest projects – and in a wide range of styles. There was the splendid design for St George's, Southwark, in late English Gothic and with a central tower; this church was only completed, after much dispute and many changes, in 1848. There was the equally splendid church of St Michael the Archangel at Gorey in Ireland, in the Norman style; the Loreto Abbey Church at Rathfarnham, Dublin, with a beautiful lantern resembling the one at Ely Cathedral; and there was St Chad's Cathedral, Birmingham.

The exterior of this, the first Catholic cathedral to be built in England since the Reformation, was based on the Gothic of Munich Cathedral. Again this was probably for reasons of economy – it enabled it to be built in brick – and a newspaper report described it as 'a mass of perforated brick walls and high roofs'. The effect is rather of a model cathedral cast in metal: a little angular and plain, but neat and incisive. Rich decoration and painted stone were reserved for the interior in accordance with Pugin's priorities. The roof of the crossing is decorated with the most delicate painted and gilded diaper, the columns soar to support a roof eighty feet above the ground – for in spite of the comparison of the exterior to a model, it is a vast church, if not one of the larger cathedrals – and the building was studded with ecclesiastical antiquities bought by Lord Shrewsbury.

The screen, which has now gone, contained fifteenth-century carving and thirteenth-century figures of prophets, and the rood was an ancient one; the stalls were fourteenth-century German; the aisle walls were hung with old triptychs; the lectorium was a medieval treasure; and so on. Many of the architectural details resemble old examples: the portal with its figure of the Virgin; the figures of saints on the west front; the doors like those of Lichfield and York; corbels and foliage after the 'original authorities'; sedilia after those in Westminster Abbey; and – to take advantage of a rise in the ground – a crypt decorated in 'the true style of Christian art'. An unusual feature for Pugin was 'a loft for choristers' at the west end. The result of all this was not imitation: Pugin worked the various elements into a harmony which was his own and which he drew into a lofty structure full of space and drama, 'purple with stained glass and rich with gilding'. It is a work of which Pugin was justly proud, though he acknowledged its 'defects . . . as his own', and gave credit for the rest to 'the glorious race of old Catholic artists'.

Pugin was ill in the February of 1841 and had to drive himself to finish St Chad's. He was unwell for the dedication ceremony in June, and again a few months later. His sight was failing through iritis, and he was weakened by the mercury drug prescribed for this disease and by bleeding. From now on Pugin was never fully well. He was still working on his long-standing projects, however, and was also designing houses as well as a convent at Bermondsey, the first of many such undertakings.

By 1841 Irish commissions had become important. They included one for the chapel of St Peter's College, Wexford, which is basically in Pugin's early style, and is enlivened by a large round window and an elaborate triptych altar. But the major work of this time is St Michael's, Gorey, begun in 1839 and consecrated in 1842. In common with most of Pugin's Irish work it is large – almost as large as St Chad's. It was Pugin's first cruciform or basilican church and was built without the spire shown in the frontispiece to the *Apology*. Instead it has a massive tower, and the exterior, with its hewn stone, is bold and striking. This is partly due to the availability of skilled and relatively cheap labour – a factor which contributed to the success of most of Pugin's Irish work, which is generally marked by excellence of building and rugged simplicity. Pugin was well served by his builders both in England, where he often relied on George Myers, and here in Ireland, where he was helped by Robert Pierce.

Fine as the exterior is, it is the interior of St Michael's which is wonderful: dark, almost catacomb-like, with ranks of plain Norman arches picked out as sharp crescents of light on dark, and vistas of slender, powerful arcade columns of Wicklow granite gleaming in the shadow and intersecting at the crossing. In this achievement Pugin showed himself deeply in sympathy not only with Gothic, but with any architectural integrity, including the ancient building of Ireland.

Pugin also designed the parish churches at Tagoat and

St Giles', Cheadle (left), and St George's, Southwark, from Pugin's
'Present State of Ecclesiastical Architecture'. St Giles' is a measure of
Pugin's achievement and to this church he devoted six years of his life.

Barntown in Wexford. Both churches are simple on the outside
and impressive within – Barntown, in particular, having a
well-knit exterior and a fine, sombre interior. In 1841 Pugin
said of his stay in Ireland: 'as far as the poor people are
concerned I have been greatly edified . . . for the rich I can say
little'.

In 1839 Pugin had devised his first plans for Downside
College. They were never executed. But by that time, and in the
space of about four years, Pugin had become established as an
architect, as an authority on Gothic and Roman Catholic
architecture, as a promulgator of Roman Catholicism and as a
leader of taste, and in 1840, when Pugin was twenty-eight, the
Papacy thanked him for his 'exertions' in these directions. The
Gothic Revival had begun before Pugin appeared on the scene,
but by his passionate and Catholic conviction he was in the
process of giving it a new intensity; he saw Gothic not as

something to be applied, but as a way of thinking and a way of expressing the spirit of religion. Pugin was developing his architectural principles, and was trying to realise them. This was not always easy and at this time he was freer to achieve exactly what he wanted in the art of designing church plate, which he practised with characteristic energy. The result was work of great richness and vigour. Elaborate designs seemed to be stored, or to spring up, in his mind with unending facility.

The *True Principles* appeared in 1841, and in the same year, the second and revised edition of *Contrasts*. Pugin knew that this edition was controversial and that a 'storm of indignation' would 'fall on' him. In the time which had elapsed since the publication of the first edition in 1836, Pugin's views had evolved through experience and religious and liturgical scholarship, and it is interesting to note the painters and thinkers he cites as the best representatives of Christian ideals: Overbeck, Giotto, Orcagna, Fra Angelico, Perugino and Raphael on the one hand; and Durandus, J. B. Thiers, Montalembert, Rio and Savonarola on the other.

In 1840 Pugin had designed four major churches, St Giles', Cheadle, St George's, Southwark, St Mary's, Stockton-on-Tees, and St Oswald's, Liverpool, and one exquisite small church, St Mary's, Warwick Bridge, Cumberland. All of these were now being built. St Mary's, Warwick Bridge, has a modest exterior and since it is also of local stone it blends well with the other buildings in the area, in the way that Pugin had learned in Ireland. The interior is unexpected – a miniature complete with the most delicate colour and gilding and ornament.

Pugin had to abandon his original design for St George's and to transfer the tower from the centre to the west. The result was an impressive church, but it was not such a beautiful and balanced solution as the first would have been to the problem of the site, which was triangular. Because of this shape, and because room had to be provided for 3,000 people, the nave is nearly three times as long as the church is wide. With these reservations, Pugin was justified in calling it a 'great' church. St Oswald's, opened in 1842 and since replaced by a larger church, was a fine-looking building, a simpler version of the one that stands today as one of Pugin's most splendid achievements – St Giles', Cheadle.

The parish church of St Giles is like a treasure chest,

massive in its proportions, and with an interior full of richly coloured decoration, including painted stonework, a painting of the Doom done in Rome, Minton's tiles, stained glass made by Wailes, screens of 'brass and gilt wood', £1,000 worth of Pugin's and Hardman's plate and metalwork, and a fifteenth-century Flemish corona in a sanctuary bedizened with diaper and gilt. A door with the heraldic lions of the arms of Shrewsbury seals the west end of the church and religious symbolism is everywhere. It took Pugin six years to build and at the end of this time, in 1846, his health was very poor indeed. St Giles' cost Lord Shrewsbury – for it was a special and local venture of his – at least '£30,000 or £40,000' and he never embarked on such an ambitious undertaking again. It was based on a study of the large parish churches of Norfolk, and it also incorporates some continental features, but, as usual, the result is new and idiosyncratic. The liturgical arrangements are exactly as Pugin desired, he had made the church as splendid as he could, and with one or two reservations, when it was finished he could say 'Perfect Cheadle, Cheadle my consolation in all my afflictions'.

By the time St Giles' was finished the length of the nave was about one and a half times the width of the church, and with exceptions such as St George's, Southwark, this satisfying ratio became the standard one for Pugin's later churches – his earlier ones were often far more elongated. Pugin's grasp of design was now assured and mature: he could design large churches with all the authority they required. In the years from 1840 he produced plans for St Barnabas' Cathedral, Nottingham; Killarney Cathedral; Enniscorthy Cathedral (in 1843); and the monastery at Mount St Bernard. All are cruciform. Mount St Bernard was conceived by March-Phillipps as an attempt to 'revive the monastic spirit'. He poured a considerable sum of money into the project, but was unable to complete it until Lord Shrewsbury gave assistance – and it never was completed in Pugin's lifetime. Pugin himself took nothing for his work. The building is beautiful, with its 'solid simplicity . . . thick walls and lancet windows', and Pugin was right when he said that 'the building already possesses the appearance of antiquity'. It thus satisfied something in his nature, as well as March-Phillipps' purpose, for he found 'the mind . . . forcibly carried back to the days of England's faith'.

St Barnabas', planned in 1841, cost £15,000 to build and

✠ Frontals for Altars &c.

most of this was paid by Lord Shrewsbury. For this, Pugin gave him a stone church one fifth longer than St Chad's, Birmingham, and, as Pugin said, one with 'a grand appearance, although *perfectly plain'* and with 'a most solemn and rich interior'. But for majesty and power, it cannot compete with Enniscorthy and, above all, with Killarney. The exterior masses of this are splendidly composed and proportioned, the stone is rugged, and the detail is at once strong and delicate enough to continue the sense of harmony. The building seems to blend with the surrounding land, and with Ireland's architectural and religious past. The same unity is observed within: simplicity, and a lofty, echoing austerity are preserved by serried arcades, and the three towering lancets at the east end. The building of Killarney, begun in 1842, was interrupted by the Irish Famine, and only resumed in 1850, so that Pugin did not live to see its completion. Enniscorthy is as large as Killarney and has many of the same qualities of simplicity and strength. It is an extremely imposing building – but it lacks the final grandeur of Killarney.

LATE CHURCHES, RESTORATION AND OTHER WORK
With St Mary's, Stockton-on-Tees, Pugin's church-building entered a new phase. Most of the eighteen churches he designed after 1841 were asymmetrical, and relatively small and lacking in ornament; in some ways they approximated to the ordinary parish church. Only a handful of the asymmetrical churches, however, are successful: St Marie's, Liverpool, St Peter's, Marlow, St Thomas of Canterbury, Fulham – a handsome church this – and above all, St Augustine's, Ramsgate. This is Pugin's own church, designed towards the end of his life, and neither he nor his helpers John Hardman and George Myers spared any pains to make it a beautiful building, richly furnished, well-proportioned, and natural to its Kentish setting. By comparison St Peter's, Woolwich, and the Cathedral Church of St Mary, Newcastle, are almost ungainly.

Even if Pugin's wish to experiment produced rather mixed results, it was a mark of his spirit, and he was led to it by his own observations. But the idea of asymmetrical planning was in the air, and was also adopted by the Cambridge Camden

Opposite: three designs for altar frontals, from Pugin's 'Glossary of Ecclesiastical Ornament', 1844.

Society, or Ecclesiological Society as it later became. This led to a temporary accord between Pugin and the Society, but the Society's members were Protestant, and some of them eventually attacked him as a 'Schismatick' who was 'indifferent to Symbolism in architecture'. Nothing could have been less true and Pugin was 'grieved'.

Pugin also emerged as a master of 'restoration', though in some cases his additions were extensive. The best instances are the Rolle Chantry, Bicton, the collegiate chapels at Ware and Ushaw, and the Protestant St Mary's, West Tofts, which all show Pugin's decorative brilliance and structural instinct. The work at these places is related to a book Pugin published in 1849, *Floriated Ornament*.

Throughout his architectural practice, Pugin designed many other kinds of religious building. St Giles', St Oswald's and St George's had their own educational and conventual buildings, and Pugin designed convents at Alton, Birmingham (1840), Nottingham and Liverpool, and at Waterford, Gorey and Birr in Ireland. He was responsible for the Bishop's House in Birmingham, Ratcliffe College, Leicestershire, the massive Maynooth College near Dublin, St Anne's Bedehouses in Lincoln, and a host of presbyteries – and schools, such as the fine one at Spetchley, Worcestershire. This is informal and domestic in character, as is most of Pugin's auxiliary religious building, certainly in the best cases such as Mount St Bernard, though several of the examples mentioned are more reserved, and slightly dispiriting.

This criticism does not apply to Pugin's purely domestic architecture. Here he excelled himself, as the fine stone Glebe Farm, Rampisham, Dorset, shows. He designed dozens of smaller houses and could have specialised in them alone. He also built The Grange at Ramsgate for himself and his family in 1843–44, and in due course they settled there. It is an ample and serviceable brick house, set on a cliff top. It is certainly not extravagant, but its tower, oriel window, tall chimneys and stained glass give it a medieval air.

Pugin had an astonishing aptitude, refined by practice and scholarship, for designing ornament and fittings of all kinds, and this aspect of his activities became increasingly important as his career advanced. The metalwork business he had entered into with Hardman flourished, and in 1849 the orders totalled

£14,500. Pugin was constantly adding new designs, as well as acting as an agent and attending to problems of manufacture. In the mid 1840s the firm started making stained glass and Pugin established a workshop at his own house in Ramsgate, a move he sometimes regretted when he wanted privacy. But it too became extremely busy. Then there was J. G. Crace, who made furniture, wallpaper and fabric to Pugin's designs and fitted out whole interiors to his specifications, and the builder George Myers, who also made furniture and provided other forms of carved work as well. Bookbinding, embroidery, tiles, wall painting – the list of Pugin's interests seems endless: everyone seemed to want to tap his inventive powers while they lasted. Other architects used his metalwork and stained glass and among them were R. C. Carpenter, William Butterfield, and Penson. After 1844 Pugin was once again preparing thousands of drawings for the decoration of the Houses of Parliament.

THE 'APOLOGY'

In 1843 Pugin produced his last major book, *An Apology for the Revival of Christian Architecture in England*. It was dedicated to Lord Shrewsbury, and in it Pugin attacks the contemporary 'carnival of architecture', whose 'professors appear tricked out in the guises of all centuries and all nations'.

On the positive side, the *Apology* sought 'to place Christian architecture in its true position – to exhibit the claims it possesses on our veneration and obedience, as the only correct expression of the faith, wants, and climate of our country.' The appeal was not to beauty alone, but to principle and suitability – though 'suitability' is a mild word for what was to Pugin an article of faith. 'Pagan', Classic works Pugin believed 'to be the perfect expressions of imperfect systems: the summit of human skill, expended on human inventions' and feelings; but Gothic was the perfect expression of 'all we should hold sacred, honourable, and national'.

Last years

ADVERSITY
1843 marked the beginning of a difficult period for Pugin. His practice was flourishing, and the next year saw the publication of his splendid *Glossary of Ecclesiastical Ornament*. But the beautiful designs he produced for the rebuilding at Balliol College, Oxford, some of which are kept at the College in an illuminated book bound in red velvet and brass, were turned down, on the ironic ground that Pugin was a Catholic – for Balliol is a medieval Catholic foundation. Since he had found the project 'almost too exciting to bear' this was a deep disappointment. He also now had to compete for Catholic commissions with other architects – among them Charles Hansom and Matthew Hadfield.

On the other hand, his wife Louisa had been converted to Catholicism, and the Pugins now had six children: Anne, the eldest (twelve), Edward Welby, Agnes, Cuthbert, Katherine, and Mary, still less than a year old. But in August 1844 Louisa Pugin died. Pugin was grief-stricken, and soon afterwards he moved with his children to The Grange at Ramsgate.

By 1846 Pugin's health was much worse, so that he feared for his life: iritis persisted, he had a kidney disease, and he was 'suffering from a most severe illness, produced by anxiety of mind'. He was aided in his recovery from this by a girl of twenty-five, and eventually they became engaged. Pugin settled his property in her favour, got The Grange ready for her reception and had many dresses and pieces of jewellery made for her – in a flurry of activity: 'I do trust everything will please you . . . I have between thirty and forty people working different ways. There are five at your jewellery at Birmingham; of course I cannot pretend to vie in intrinsic value with thousands of people; but no woman, not excepting the Queen, will have better ornaments, as regards taste, than you will'.

Pugin wrote that he 'had loved her in secret for a

42

considerable time' before he mentioned his affection to her. At the last minute, she broke off the engagement. Pugin supposed that this was a result of her family's, and especially her father's, violent opposition to Catholicism. The girl had become a convert and they had stopped her attending Mass, but she herself, Pugin wrote, had added 'insult to injury'. The whole incident was 'destructive to (his) peace of mind', and he was so outraged that he published all these details in a pamphlet for private circulation: *A Statement of Facts relative to the Engagement of marriage between Miss (. . .), and Augustus Welby Pugin, Esq. of S. Augustins, Isle of Thanet.* It was certainly one of the stranger episodes of his life.

THE THIRD MARRIAGE

Pugin did eventually get married again – in 1848, to Jane Knill. They had two children, and Pugin called her 'a first-rate Gothic woman . . . who perfectly understands and delights in spires, chancels, screens, stained windows, brasses, vestments, etc.' But before this marriage Pugin had had two more abortive engagements. In the first case he was not considered a good enough match for the girl and in the second the girl was not considered a good enough match for him. Pugin was also under frequent attack from magazines such as *The Ecclesiologist*, and as mentioned earlier he entered into frustrating controversies over the matter of rood-screens, which were now becoming increasingly dear to him, and his study of which culminated in 1851 in *A Treatise on Chancel Screens and Rood Lofts, their antiquity, use and symbolic signification.*

THE HOUSES OF PARLIAMENT

Undoubtedly one of the major burdens of Pugin's last years was the work he did on the Houses of Parliament in response to Barry's renewed and repeated appeals for help, which began a few weeks after Louisa's death in 1844. After both Pugin and Barry were dead, Edward Pugin and Alfred Barry conducted a dispute in pamphlet form about the extent of their fathers' contributions to the building. Each was led to the extreme of claiming almost sole authorship on his father's behalf. This was a legacy of the ill-feeling that had existed between Pugin and Barry, and of the fact that even though Pugin was now, on his own insistence, employed by the Government and not by Barry, he was still not adequately rewarded or recognised for his efforts. Apart from the salary Pugin drew as Superintendent of the Works, Edward Pugin estimated that his father gained only £3,000 or £4,000 for eight years of concentrated and arduous work on the most important secular building in the land. Edward probably also felt that Barry had helped to work Pugin to death – though it is likely that Pugin's temperament would anyhow have found other work to burn its way through.

Although Barry was not Pugin's employer, his requests were still peremptory, slightly condescending, and ceaseless. In 1851 and 1852, when Barry was overworked and Pugin was near the limit of his endurance, order after order arrived: for a 'hexagon pump in the cloisters', 'inkstands of proper mediæval character', paper holders, 'wall tiles for the smoking room', chandeliers, a cloak stand, 'details for the gates' and 'furniture for the official residences'. In the middle of this work Pugin suffered a 'severe attack of nervous fever' which prevented his 'returning too quickly to anything that requires much mental exertion'. Barry was solicitous, but nevertheless the orders were soon pouring in again: for 'fifteen boxes for letters', 'small interlaced patterns for papers', metal guards for fires and rosaces 'for filling a ventilation hole'; for blotting cases, 'simple candlesticks', ink-holders, and 'varieties of beasts or cognizances'; and for 'eighteen umbrella stands . . . of quaint design'. Barry was certainly a brilliant organiser, and Pugin a willing horse, and therein lies the answer to the puzzle of the disputed authorship. The answer is plain for us to see: the planning and committee-work were Barry's, the vast amount of decorative detail was Pugin's. Its effect is brilliant – coherent, inventive, splendid – and his masterpiece in this respect is the interior of the House of Lords, a building for which he said he produced two thousand designs.

THE GREAT EXHIBITION

Apart from his contribution to the Houses of Parliament, the last public work Pugin undertook was as a Commissioner of Fine Arts for the Great Exhibition of 1851. He was responsible for the Medieval Court and an observer has left this description: 'The exhibitors . . . had in view the illustration of a style of decoration now almost totally neglected except in Roman Catholic churches . . . On his entrance, the visitor was struck with the awe which is so often felt in a sanctuary: the place was, as it were, set apart from the rest of the Exhibition, looking dark and solemn for the display of the taste and art of dead men.' The exhibitors were mainly Pugin and his associates Hardman, Myers and Minton, and the objects they displayed included all the things at which they had become adept, as well as one or two curiosities such as a huge stove in medieval style, and the jewellery Pugin had designed for the girl who had broken off their engagement some four years previously.

DEATH

By the end of 1851 Pugin was extremely ill and distressed. He began to imagine things – that several ships had just been wrecked outside Ramsgate harbour, for example, or that 'there was now but one Church'. On occasion he even acted upon his fantasies, as when he made out imaginary cheques for the local poor. At the beginning of 1852 he again fell victim to kidney disease and to attacks of partial blindness. He alternated between periods of mental and physical suffering which reduced him to inactivity – an added blow – and periods of intense creativity, in which he corresponded enthusiastically about tiles Minton was making to his designs, and planned what was to be a new and radical work, *An Apology for the separated Church of England since the reign of the Eighth Henry.*

Finally Pugin became insane and violent. He was 'removed to the Golden Cross in Wellington Street, Strand, and put under proper restraint', though he attacked George Myers when he paid him a visit. His violence increased and he was transferred to the Bethlehem Hospital. There was something of an outcry at this, and Mrs Pugin, who had cared for him almost from the day they were married, saw to it that he was moved to a private house in The Grove, Hammersmith. He seemed a little better and on 11th September 1852 he was taken back to The Grange at Ramsgate. For a day or so he was almost his old self, and seemed restored by his surroundings, but on 14th September, after a night of violent convulsions, he died. He was buried in the Pugin Chantry of his church of St Augustine, Ramsgate.

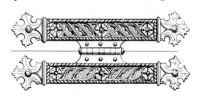

THE PRINCIPAL EVENTS OF PUGIN'S LIFE

1812   Pugin born
1824   Makes architectural trip to Paris with father
1826   Surveys Rochester Castle
1827   Designs furniture for Windsor Castle, and plate for Rundell and Bridge (goldsmiths)
1830   Opens stone-carving business at Hart Street, London. *King William IV succeeds George IV*
1831   Marries Ann Garnett. Designs scenery for 'Kenilworth'
1832   Ann Pugin dies in childbirth. Pugin's father dies
1833   Pugin's mother dies. Marries Louisa Burton
1834   Birth of first son, Edward Welby. *Houses of Parliament burned*
1835   Pugin converted to Roman Catholicism. Builds St Marie's Grange at Salisbury. Begins work with Charles Barry on winning designs for new Houses of Parliament. *Gothic Furniture in the Style of the Fifteenth Century*
1836   *Contrasts.* Introduced to Lord Shrewsbury. *Designs for Gold and Silversmiths. Designs for Iron and Brass Work in the style of the XV and XVI centuries. Details of antient houses of the 15th and 16th centuries*
1837   Begins work on Alton Towers and Scarisbrick Hall. Appointed Architect and Professor of Ecclesiastical Antiquities at Oscott College. Meets Ambrose March-Phillipps. *Queen Victoria succeeds William IV*
1839   Completes first church: St Mary's, Uttoxeter
1841   *The True Principles of Pointed or Christian Architecture.* Dedication of St Chad's, Birmingham
1843   *An Apology for The Revival of Christian Architecture in England*
1844   Louisa Pugin dies. Renews work on the Houses of Parliament. The Grange, Ramsgate, completed. *Glossary of Ecclesiastical Ornament and Costume*
1847   Visits Rome for first time. Audience with Pope and is presented with gold medal in recognition of services
1848   Marries Jane Knill. St George's, Southwark, opened
1849   *Floriated Ornament*
1850   St Augustine's, Ramsgate, completed
1851   Commissioner of Fine Arts for the Great Exhibition. *A Treatise on Chancel Screens and Rood Lofts*
1852   Goes insane and dies at Ramsgate

WHERE TO SEE PUGIN'S WORKS

Pugin's work may be seen at a great many places all over Britain. The following county list of a few of his more completely remaining works includes, as shown in brackets, examples of his architecture, furniture and decoration.

Berkshire: St James Church, Reading (arch.); church, rectory and school at Tubney (arch. and dec.). *Cheshire:* St Alban's Church, Macclesfield (arch.). *Cumberland:* St Mary's, Warwick Bridge (arch.). *Derbyshire:* Burton Close, Bakewell (arch. and dec.); St Mary's Church, Derby (arch.). *Dorset:* farm, school and church at Rampisham (arch. and furn.). *Durham:* St Mary's, Stockton-on-Tees (arch.). *Hertfordshire:* St Edmund's College, Ware (arch. and furn.). *Kent:* St Augustine's Church, Ramsgate (arch.); The Grange, Ramsgate (Pugin's own house). *Lancashire:* Scarisbrick Hall, Ormskirk (arch.). *Leicestershire:* Garendon and Grace Dieu Houses (arch. and furn.); Mount St Bernard's Abbey (arch.); St Mary's, Wymeswold (arch. and furn.). *Lincolnshire:* St Swithin's Church, Leadenham (dec.). *London:* Houses of Parliament (dec.); Our Lady Star of the Sea, Greenwich (dec.); St Thomas of Canterbury Church, Fulham (arch. and furn.). *Northumberland:* Cathedral Church of St Mary, Newcastle-upon-Tyne (arch. and furn.). *Nottinghamshire:* Cathedral Church of St Barnabas, Nottingham (arch.); Convent of Mercy, Nottingham (arch. and furn.). *Oxfordshire:* St John's Church, Banbury (arch.). *Staffordshire:* Alton Church and Alton Towers (arch.); St Giles Church, school, convent and presbytery at Cheadle (arch.); St Mary's Church, presbytery and school at Brewood (arch.). *Surrey:* SS Peter and Paul Church, and Albury House, at Albury (arch. and dec.). *Warwickshire:* Aston cemetery chapel, Birmingham (arch.); Bilton Grange, Rugby (arch.); Erdington Abbey (dec.); Metropolitan Cathedral Church of St Chad's, Birmingham (arch.); Oscott College, Sutton Coldfield (arch., dec. and drawings); St Augustine's Church and presbytery at Kenilworth (arch.); St Augustine's Church, Solihull (arch.). *Wiltshire:* St Osmund's Church, Salisbury (arch. and furn.). *Worcestershire:* Our Blessed Lady and St Alphonsus Church, Blackmore Park (metalwork); Our Lady and St Thomas of Canterbury Church, Dudley (arch.). *Yorkshire:* Ackworth Grange, Pontefract (arch. and tiles); Cathedral Church of St Anne, Leeds (furn.); St Mary's Church, Beverley (arch., furn. and dec.).

47

INDEX
Page numbers in italic refer to illustrations